Many Leaves

by Ann Rossi

PEARSON
Scott
Foresman

What You Already Know

Chameleons use camouflage to stay safe.

Animals live in different habitats. Animal body parts help them live. Animals use their body parts to help them find food. Animals also have ways to stay safe where they live.

Animals have many ways to stay safe. Sometimes they help each other. Sometimes they use camouflage.

Plants are different from animals. Plants have different parts than animals do. Their parts help them live in different habitats too.

Plants have parts. Roots take in water. They also hold the plant in the ground. The stem moves water around the plant. The leaf makes food. The flower makes seeds. Plants have different kinds of leaves.

Plant parts help plants stay safe. Some plants use camouflage too.

In this book, you will learn about leaves that live in different places. You will find out that different leaves help plants live in different kinds of places.

Leaf Life

There are many different kinds of leaves. Leaves grow in many places in the world. They have special parts to help them live in all these places.

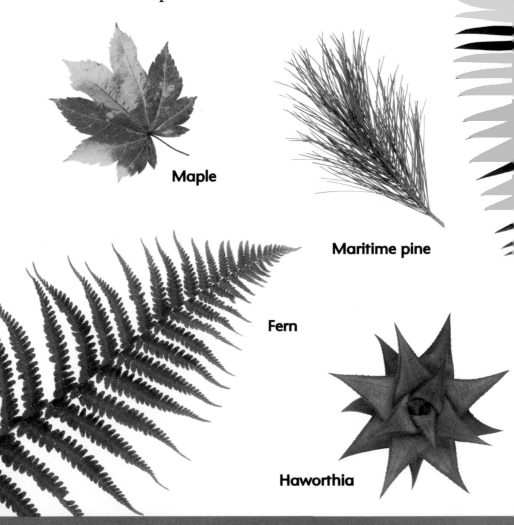

Maple

Maritime pine

Fern

Haworthia

Fanwort

Eucalyptus

Rattan palm

Leaves come in many shapes, sizes, and colors. Some are as small as a baby's little toe. But some are as long as a bus! You will see many kinds of leaves on these pages.

Woodland Leaves

Many kinds of leaves grow in woodlands. Woodlands are places with lots of trees. Some woodland trees have simple leaves. A simple leaf is one leaf on one stem. Other woodland trees have compound leaves. A compound leaf has many leaves on one stem.

Norway maple

Fern

Ash

Oak

Beech

Maple leaves

Some leaves change color in the fall. This happens when the days are short. The leaves fall to the ground by winter. New leaves grow in spring.

Evergreens stay green all year. They grow new leaves as they shed their old ones. Holly and laurel are evergreens. So are most conifers. Conifers are plants that have cones. Maybe you have seen a pinecone from a conifer.

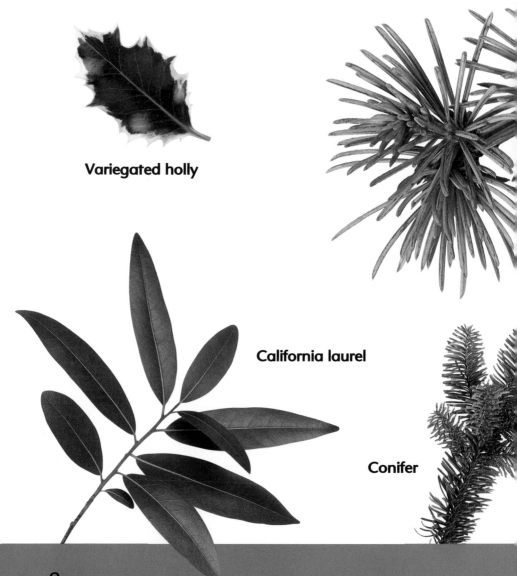

Variegated holly

California laurel

Conifer

Atlas cedar

Maritime pine

Many evergreens have small leaves with points. These leaves are better for living where it is cold. It is hard to keep water in cold, dry places. This keeps water in.

Tropical Leaves

The tropics are hot and wet places. The weather is perfect for palm plants. Most palms have leaves that look like fans or feathers. Some palm leaves are very big.

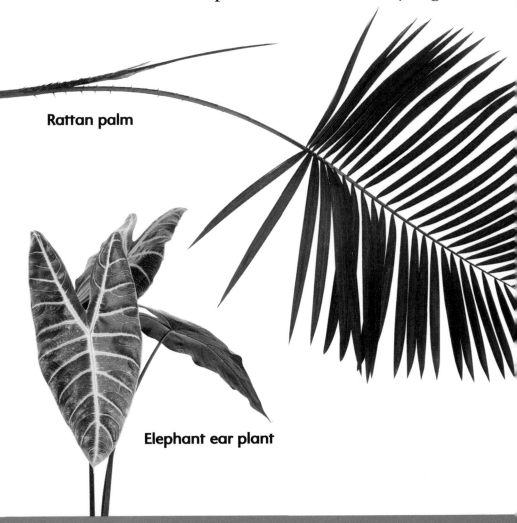

Rattan palm

Elephant ear plant

Embauba

Swiss cheese plant

Rain forests and jungles are in the tropics. Their treetops make a thick cover. Not much light from the Sun gets to the forest floor. Leaves that grow under the cover can be very large. Their size helps them get enough light to make food.

Desert Leaves

Many desert plants have small spines.
These leaves do not give off much water.
Spines also keep plants safe from animals
that want to eat them.

Eucalyptus

Desert rose

Camelthorn
acacia

Haworthia

Kokerboom

It is hard to keep water in hot, dry places. Some plants store water in thick, waxy leaves. The waxy leaves help keep water inside the plant.

Watery Leaves

Leaves that grow in water can be big or small. The flat, wide leaves of the water lily float on water. The giant water lily can grow to be as big as a car!

Mare's-tail

Water hyacinth

Fanwort

Water lily

The next time you see a plant, look at its leaves. See their size, shape, and color. Then think about how the leaves, big or small, help the plant to live.

Glossary

compound   made of more than one part

conifer   a tree that grows cones

evergreen   a plant that has green leaves all year long

float   stay up on top of water

simple   having one part or only a few parts

spines   hard plant parts with sharp points